GOAL!
LATIN STARS OF
SOCCER

Soccer Star
Andrés Iniesta

Jeff
Burlingame

Library of Congress Cataloging-in-Publication Data

Burlingame, Jeff.

Soccer star Andrés Iniesta / Jeff Burlingame.

pages cm. — (Goal! Latin stars of soccer)

Includes bibliographical references and index.

Summary: "A star player with the Spain national team and F.C. Barcelona, Andrés Iniesta was destined to be one of the greats. This sports biography explores the life of the Spanish footballer and his rise from being captain of Barcelona's Under-15 team to a key member of Barcelona's championship winning first team"—Provided by publisher.

ISBN 978-1-62285-225-3

1. Iniesta Luján , Andrés, 1984- 2. Soccer players—Spain—Barcelona—Biography—Juvenile literature. I. Title.

GV942.7.I68B87 2014

796.334092—dc23

[B]

2013014230

Future Editions:
Paperback ISBN: 978-1-62285-226-0
EPUB ISBN: 978-1-62285-227-7
Single-User PDF ISBN: 978-1-62285-228-4
Multi-User PDF ISBN: 978-1-62285-229-1

Printed in the United States of America
112013 Bang Printing, Brainerd, Minn.
10 9 8 7 6 5 4 3 2 1

To Our Readers: We have done our best to make sure all Internet addresses in this book were active and appropriate when we went to press. However, the author and the Publisher have no control over, and assume no liability for, the material available on those Internet sites or on other Web sites they may link to. Any comments or suggestions can be sent by e-mail to comments@speedingstar.com or to the address listed below.

Speeding Star
Box 398, 40 Industrial Road
Berkeley Heights, NJ 07922
USA
www.speedingstar.com

Photo Credits: ©AP Images/Andres Kudacki, pp. 20, 32; ©AP Images/Bernat Armangue, p. 11; ©AP Images/David Ramos, p. 33; ©AP Images/Eugene Hoshiko, p. 7; ©AP Images/Felice Calabro', p. 13; ©AP Images/Jon Super, p. 24; ©AP Images/Lalo R. Villar, p. 43; ©AP Images/Manu Fernandez, pp. 14, 17, 27, 31; ©AP Images/Luca Bruno, p. 40; ©AP Images/Manu Fernandez/Martin Meissner, p. 8; ©AP Images/Martin Meissner, pp. 4, 35; ©AP Images/Michael Probst, p. 28; ©AP Images/Miquel Benitez/Rex Features, p. 36; ©AP Images/Paul White, p. 23; ©AP Images/Paulo Duarte, p. 19.

Cover Photo: ©AP Images/Manu Fernandez

CONTENTS

With the championship on the line, Iniesta, left, does whatever it takes to help his team take home the trophy.

Humble Hero

For ninety minutes, the 84,490 fans at Soccer City Stadium in Johannesburg, South Africa, patiently waited for a goal that never came.

The 2010 Fédération Internationale de Football Association (FIFA) World Cup final match between Spain and the Netherlands, as the crowd witnessed, was heading into extra time. It was sudden death. The first team to score a goal would be declared the winner. Soccer fans—those inside the stadium and the hundreds of millions across the world watching on television that July 11th—had to wait a little longer before the month-long tournament would crown its world champion.

Twenty-six of the game's extra thirty minutes also ticked away without a goal. In four minutes, what had been an ugly, penalty-filled final match, would need to be decided by a shootout. Each team would get five free kicks, and the one to push the most of them past the opponent's goalkeeper and into the net would win. No one wanted such an important match to end that way. There is an element of luck to shootouts. And sometimes the team most observers consider to be the best may not be the one that comes out on top.

Fortunately, at least for those rooting for Spain, penalty kicks were not necessary this time. After stopping a scoring opportunity by the Netherlands with less than five minutes remaining, Spain quickly pressed the ball upfield. When it reached the Netherlands' end, Fernando Torres tried to pass across the field to teammate Andrés Iniesta. The ball was deflected but bounced to Spain's Cesc Fàbregas. Fàbregas maneuvered and delivered the ball to its original target, Iniesta. From there, history was made.

Iniesta gathered the ball with his feet as he pressed toward the Netherlands' goalie, Maarten Stekelenburg. Then he hammered a right-footed shot past the goalie and into the back of the net. Arms flapping wildly in celebration, Iniesta immediately removed his dark blue No. 6 jersey and ran toward the corner of the field. Underneath the jersey, Spain's new hero wore a sleeveless white T-shirt with five words handwritten on the front in Spanish: DANI JARQUE SIEMPRE CON NOSOTROS. The message—which translated to "Dani Jarque always with us"—was Iniesta's tribute to his former teammate, Dani Jarque. Jarque had died a year earlier of a heart attack at age twenty-six. "I wanted to carry Dani with me and with my other teammates," Iniesta said after the game. "We wanted to feel his strength. We wanted to pay tribute to him—and this was the best opportunity to do so. This is for Dani, for my family, for all of the people. It is the result of hard work over a long time and some difficult moments."

Spain's World Cup win definitely had been a long time coming. The country had long been considered one of the

...niesta scored the winning goal against the Netherlands to win the 2010 FIFA World Cup.

most powerful soccer nations in the world. Yet Spain had never won a World Cup. This had led many observers to label the team underachievers. Spain also had some difficult moments just getting to the title game. The team lost its first match of the tournament and only scored one goal in each of its final four games, including the championship.

Scoring that final goal with hundreds of millions of people watching had a huge impact on Iniesta. He had been a star before, but now soccer fans across the world knew his name. Still, after winning the match, the twenty-six-year-old Iniesta somehow remained humble. "I've made a small contribution in a very tough game," he said. Then, in Spain's locker room, Iniesta fell to his knees and cried.

After scoring the winning goal in the World Cup finals, Iniesta celebrates by running with a shirt that says "DANI JARQUE SIEMPRE CON NOSOTROS"— which in English means "Dani Jarque, always with us."

Moving Out, Moving Up

Andrés Iniesta Luján was born May 11, 1984, in Fuentealbilla, Spain. His birthplace was a small village in the province of Albacete in the community of La Mancha, a windy plateau in Southeastern Spain best known as the setting for the influential book *Don Quixote* by Miguel de Cervantes.

When Andrés was born, most of those living in La Mancha either earned their living off the land by growing grapes and wheat and raising sheep and cattle, working at one of the area's many manufacturing plants, or by working in the service industry selling goods and food. Andrés's father, José Antonio, worked as a bricklayer. Andrés's mother, Maria, worked as a maid. The parents also had second jobs working at a small pub owned by Andrés's grandfather called Bar Luján.

In fact, the whole Iniesta family—aunts, uncles, siblings, and cousins—chipped in at the pub when they were not in school or working at their primary jobs. Andrés's family includes one sister, Maribel, who is two years younger than her big brother. Like the rest of her family, Maribel also helped at the pub as soon as she was old enough to do so.

Most of the time, however, Andrés Iniesta was not interested in helping with the family business. He loved playing the video games in the pub but did not care much for doing the work. His mind, instead, was always on fútbol, the sport which in the United States is better known as soccer. Andrés's love of soccer came from his father. José Antonio had played soccer for various club teams throughout his life.

Growing up, Andrés rarely was without a soccer ball at his feet. He dribbled the ball everywhere and often could be found next to Bar Lujan kicking the ball off the walls of buildings and through the adjacent empty parking lot. "I always had an excuse to play with the football," Andrés later wrote on his Web site, *AndresIniesta.es*. "[T]he truth is I always carried it with me anywhere I went; it was my best friend, and the school's football field was where we spent most time together."

Andrés's talent for soccer was evident early on. He soon began playing on various teams. He started by playing futsal, a faster-paced version of soccer played on a small field or indoors with five players on a team.

When Andrés was eight years old, his parents signed him up to play for the Albacete Balompié youth soccer team. One of his parents—or other relatives—had to drive him forty-five minutes each way to practice. Some days, Andrés had to leave school at lunchtime to attend, then would return to school when practice was done. "The truth is, it was exhausting," Andrés wrote on his Web site. "But if I'm honest, I was very happy. My love for football comes deep from my heart."

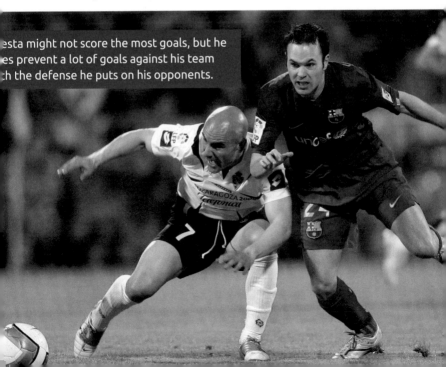

esta might not score the most goals, but he es prevent a lot of goals against his team h the defense he puts on his opponents.

Albacete Balompié was a top-level team. Andrés was on the club's junior team, but he used to spend a lot of time watching the senior matches. "I was an Albacete supporter," *El País* newspaper quoted him as saying. "Many stories have been told, but that is the reality; my father was an athletic fan, and I liked Albacete … At the weekends, as I had a pass to play in the juniors, I went to see the [team's] matches."

Andrés soon became a star player for his youth team, and other players and coaches soon took notice of his skills. One such person was a man named Albert Benaiges, who was the director of the youth system for Fútbol Club (FC) Barcelona. The one hundred-year-old FC Barcelona was one of the most famous, popular, and successful soccer clubs in the world.

Benaiges first saw Andrés when he was twelve years old and playing in a match for Albacete Balompié in the city of Brunete. "[He was] so little, with such fair skin, and so intelligent … That's the first thing I remember about him," Benaiges told *Inside Spanish Football* in 2012. Benaiges' second thought was that he needed to get Andrés on his team. "We need to find the father of the number five, I told a delegate for my team," Benaiges said. "And that's what we did, and then we signed him!"

That signing meant Andrés would be spending his weeks living and practicing at La Masia, FC Barcelona's youth academy, with hundreds of other top young players. La Masia was located in Barcelona, Spain's second-largest

With the ballhandling skills Iniesta has, most opponents are left falling to the ground when they try to defend him.

city. The city was more than three hundred miles from Andrés's home in Fuentealbilla. Andrés was sent to live at La Masia and was only able to visit his family once or twice a month. Fuentealbilla was too far away for more frequent visits. Andrés was excited to be at La Masia, but being apart from his family was difficult. The day he first left for La Masia he could hardly stop crying. "He was very close to his family and every goodbye … would become a mini-drama," Benaiges told *Soccer America* in 2012. "Andrés would be crying and he spent a lot of time at my house, and whenever my mother sees him smiling now she always makes a joke, because she remembers how much he suffered in those days."

When his family would come to visit, Andrés's mood would dramatically improve. He wrote on his Web site, "Whenever they arrived in 'Masia' I would hug them and I was the happiest man on earth. We would spend the whole weekend together, not a second apart, and I would even sleep with them."

Benaiges wondered at times whether Andrés would be strong enough to stick with La Masia or if his homesickness would become so great that he would choose to quit and go home to Fuentealbilla. Andrés often kept to himself and wept for home, calling there every day. But he battled through and never asked to leave. He also continued to improve as a soccer player and advanced through the ranks of La Masia. In 1999, he was named captain of Barcelona's Under-15 team and led them

Iniesta, left, is shown in 2007 with teammates Bojan Krkić, Ronaldinho, and Xavi Hernández. At this point, Iniesta, Krkić, and Hernández were looked upon as the future of the organization.

to victory in the Nike Premier Cup. He even scored the winning goal in the championship game.

Barcelona's coach at the time, Llorenç Serra Ferrer, decided to reward Andrés by letting him train with the first team. The fifteen-year-old thought the coach was joking when he was told. But he was not. According to *totalBarca.com*, Ferrer said: "I wanted to reward him because he was so special. He was modest, loyal, responsible and down to earth. He had tremendous emotional maturity and was very clever. He really listened and remembered all the details."

In 2001, Andrés earned a spot on Spain's Under-16 national team and helped the team win the European Championship. One day during this time, FC Barcelona player and future manager Josep "Pep" Guardiola turned to a young star player, Xavi Hernández, while watching Andrés play. The twenty-nine-year-old Guardiola said, "You're going to retire me, but this kid's going to retire us all."

Andrés later played on the Under-19 national team which won the European title in 2004. Though he was small—only five-feet, seven-inches tall and 140 pounds—Andrés was able to excel by using his speed, intelligence, and ball-handling skills to outmaneuver opponents. He played the position of midfielder, floating in the center of the field between offense and defense. When battling bigger players, Andrés told *Four Four Two Performance*, "... I play the ball quickly on the ground. Playing a quick one-two is also very effective as bigger players are slower to react and turn. I also keep a distance from them so that I can turn quickly and we don't find ourselves going for the same ball. … If you can get the ball past them a few times using a one-two they will be more reluctant to rush in and tackle, so you have more space to play."

When Andrés turned eighteen years old in 2002, he finally found a cure for the homesickness he had been experiencing for the past six years at La Masia. His family left Fuentealbilla and moved to Barcelona with him. All the parts were now in place for the small-village soccer player to make a run at his number one goal. He wanted to be part of FC Barcelona's main team. Since he was sixteen years old he had been playing for Barcelona's B, or second, team. He wanted to move up to play for the team known throughout Spain by the motto: "Més que un club" (More than a club). That is what Barcelona had been to him since the first day he arrived at La Masia. To him it was family. And that is what it would be to him for years to come.

Height can't be that important because Iniesta and Messi, both 5-feet 7-inches tall, are considered one of the best pairs in professional soccer.

Barcelona Family

Iniesta made his debut with Barcelona's first team on October 29, 2002, in a match against FC Bruges in Belgium. It was a Champions League match and more than twenty thousand fans were there. Because Barcelona already had advanced to the next round of the tournament, coach Louis van Gaal brought a lot of the B-team players along on the trip so they could gain experience and so Barcelona's stars could rest. Iniesta was one of the B-team players. On his team's official Web site, Iniesta said he "felt very comfortable that day.... It's a dream to make your first team debut. I'd been training with them since the start of the season, and I think I played a decent game."

Iniesta played most of the 2002–03 season with Barcelona's second team but did appear in a total of ten matches with the first team. He did not score a goal with the main team, but scoring goals never was his strong suit. Unlike some of the more popular American sports such as football and basketball, there is not a lot of scoring in soccer. Nearly every game is low scoring. Scores of 1–0 or 2–1 are common, thanks in part to how big the field is. Many Americans find such games boring to watch because of this lack of scoring, but oftentimes it is because they do not understand soccer's subtle nuances. Iniesta was a master at these nuances. He could dribble between two defenders that seemed to have him cut off. He could

He doesn't score many goals, so whenever he does, Iniesta likes to do a celebration of some sort.

pass to teammates who appeared to be covered. He could control the ball as long as he wanted to. "I'm not a natural scorer," he told *Four Four Two Performance*. "But if I see an opening, I'll shoot." Iniesta sometimes did just that. He scored three goals for Barcelona's B team in 2002–03.

In 2003–04, Iniesta also split his time between the A and B teams. The following season, 2004–05, he finally became a permanent member of Barcelona's A team. His main role that season was as a backup, behind established, slightly older stars such as Xavi Hernández and Ronaldo

"Ronaldinho" de Assis Moreira, who at the time was the FIFA World Player of the Year. Still, Iniesta played in almost every game that season and scored two goals on the season. Barcelona won the league championship.

Barcelona also won the league championship the following season, with Iniesta initially filling much the same role as he had the previous campaign. He started several games that season when Hernández was injured. In the championship match in Paris against Arsenal on May 17, 2006, Iniesta started the second half and played a critical role in his team's 2–1 win.

The powers that be in Spanish soccer noticed Iniesta's continued improvement. They believed one day he could be a superstar. Still, it surprised many people when coach Luis Aragonés chose him to be a member of Spain's 2006 national team. Especially because that year, as is every fourth year, was a World Cup year. At twenty-two-years old, Iniesta was the second-youngest player on the national team. The Spanish squad made it to the final sixteen in the World Cup, then lost to France, 3–1. Iniesta only played in one game during the finals, but scored three goals during the eleven World Cup-qualifying games he played in.

The top-level, international experience Iniesta gained from playing in the World Cup helped him tremendously during Barcelona's next season. He played in fifty-six of Barcelona's matches during the 2006-07 year and scored a career-high nine goals in the process. He also switched his jersey number from 34 to his preferred number 8 that season. "[Eight] was the number I always wore [on] the underage teams," he wrote on his Web site. Around that time, some mild controversy came Iniesta's way when the Spanish newspaper *MARCA* published a story on July 19, 2007. The story suggested that Iniesta was going to switch teams, leaving Barcelona to play for archrival Real Madrid. Iniesta was shocked when he heard the news. Barcelona was family to him. He responded to the newspaper: "I've been told about that and I'm very surprised. I can't do anything about it, but I'd like to insist once again that I want to stay here. When I say I want to retire in [Barcelona], I say it with all my heart. And my wishes are above everything else."

A few months later, Iniesta proved he was serious about staying in Barcelona. He signed a contract to keep him playing there until 2015.

Iniesta still was a member of the national team in 2008, when Spain won the European Championship, 1–0, over Germany on June 29. Though ill during many of the games and had injured his knee in the final game, Iniesta played well enough to be selected to the All-Tournament team.

The honor was one of several Iniesta would win over the course of his career. His attitude toward winning such awards was one reason fans continued to fall in love with him. "I don't play to win individual awards," he told *FCBarcelona.com.*

Fans also loved Iniesta because he was the common man. He was balding and relatively small. He looked

Xavi Hernández already knew that Iniesta would be a star, even before Josep Guardiola mentioned it to him. Xavi plays with Andrés on the Spanish national team and FC Barcelona.

nothing like a typical athlete. He had no flamboyant tattoos, earrings, or fancy haircuts. Away from the game, he was shy and humble. Fans could relate to him. Iniesta has said he will always remain modest, regardless of the fame he may achieve. As he told *totalBarca.com* in 2013: "I like to return to the small town where I grew up and hang out with my old friends. It is easy for me to be me. I am how my parents educated me. I am what I am thanks to my parents. It's impossible to lose those values. When I was twelve years old my father saved money for three months to buy me [expensive soccer cleats]. I have money now, but each time I look at those [shoes] I remember where I come from."

Iniesta scores the game-tying goal against Chelsea. This goal was a big reason Barcelona moved on to the Champions League finals in 2009.

"Iniesta is the danger"

The departure of superstars Ronaldinho and Anderson "Deco" Luís de Souza prior to the start of the 2008-09 season created an opening for Iniesta. Now every game he was inked into the starting lineup as a midfielder. And he also became one of the team's captains. Iniesta did not disappoint his fans or coaches, especially when he was on the field. But that season Iniesta suffered a few minor injuries that kept him out of several games. Yet he still ended the year in spectacular fashion.

In extra time of the semifinals of the Champions League on May 6, 2009, Iniesta scored the tying goal against Chelsea. His shot curved off his foot into the upper-right corner of the net. "I connected with that shot … right from my heart, with all my might," Iniesta wrote in his 2009 book, *Un any al paradís.*

Iniesta's mighty goal helped send Barcelona to the finals in Rome against Manchester United. Prior to that championship match, Manchester's manager, Sir Alex Ferguson, said that Iniesta was the Barcelona player who frightened him most. "Iniesta is the danger," he said. "He's fantastic. He makes the team work. The way he finds passes, his movement and ability to create space is incredible." Iniesta had one assist in the final match, held in front of sixty-two thousand people at historic Stadio Olimpico. Barcelona won, 2–0. It was another championship for Iniesta and the rest of his teammates.

Despite his popularity, Iniesta was, for the most part, able to keep his personal life out of the public eye. That personal life included his relationship with girlfriend Anna Ortiz. Ortiz was a hairdresser from Catalonia, Spain, and she and Iniesta began dating in 2008. That relationship was not widely known until the next year, when pictures began to surface online of the couple vacationing on the island of Formentera in the Mediterranean Sea. The photos were snapped while Iniesta was taking some time off from soccer to recover from a thigh injury.

Barcelona's 2009–10 season—during which Iniesta tied his career-high in goals scored with nine—was another successful one. Barcelona won four major titles that season. Iniesta was considered for some major

One of the grandest trophies Iniesta has won is the 2012 UEFA Best Player in Europe award.

hardware, as well. He finished fourth place in voting for the 2009 Ballon d'Or award, given each year to the best player in the world. Lionel Messi, Iniesta's Barcelona teammate, won the award, while another teammate, Xavi Hernández, finished third. Iniesta also finished second in voting for the FIFA Puskás Award, which goes to the person who scored the best goal of the year.

Iniesta's top goal was the one he had scored against Chelsea on May 6, 2009, which sent his team to the Champions League finals. Iniesta told *FCBarcelona.com* scoring that goal was "... something I will always remember. It was one of those moments when everyone knew where

The 2010 Ballon d'Or award was special because three of the top five finalists were members of FC Barcelona. (Iniesta, Messi, and Hernández).

they were, what they were doing and how to react. I feel privileged to have scored and lived that moment. It is the maximum expression of happiness, intensity, and emotion. It's virtually impossible to beat a moment like that."

Shoemaker Nike took notice of Iniesta's successes and partnered with the Spanish star. Nike produced a pair of cleats that came with a code that allowed the purchaser to go online and get exclusive training tips from Iniesta. The American company clearly knew Iniesta's stardom was on the rise. Though, exactly how high it would go still was undetermined. After all, Iniesta was just twenty-five years old and still had not yet reached his peak as a player.

There were hardships in Iniesta's mostly charmed life, however. The biggest one came in August 2009, when his former teammate, Dani Jarque, died suddenly. The two men had played together on Spain's junior national teams for several years.

Jarque's death hit Iniesta hard: "[His] death completely changed my vision of life," he told *totalBarca.com* in 2013. "I lost my personal stability and everything around me was turned on its head. Terribly bad ideas went through my mind. Sometimes I struggle to understand what goes on in the world. Natural disasters like the floods in Australia, or the earthquake in Japan make me extremely upset. I get very down thinking about the dreadful experience some people have."

On the field, all was still rosy for the small midfielder. In 2010, he was again selected to play for the Spanish team in the World Cup. That year's event was to be held in Johannesburg, South Africa. Just as there had been four years earlier when Iniesta first played in the world championship event, thirty-two teams from across the world would be competing. Unlike how he was used in his first World Cup, however, Iniesta would not be a role player coming off the bench this time. Now he was a star, and one of the players Spain counted on to lead it to victory. In the early Group Stage, Iniesta showed he was not going to disappoint. During the game against Chile on June 25, Iniesta scored in the thirty-seventh minute. His goal turned out to be the difference in the important match, which Spain won, 2–1, in front of forty-two thousand people.

Following the win, Spain entered the knockout, or elimination, stage. The team won its first game against Portugal, its second game against Paraguay, and its third game against Germany. All of Spain's wins were by identical 1–0 scores. Those victories advanced the team to the championship match against the Netherlands, which had not scored fewer than two goals in any of its three elimination matches.

The final match between Spain and the Netherlands was billed as a special one. Both teams were perennial winners, though neither country had ever won a World Cup. The match disappointed those who wanted a lot of scoring, but it did not disappoint those who liked tension. After the first ninety minutes, the match was tied at 0. That

Iniesta celebrates with Messi after winning the 2009 UEFA Champions League title. Because of these teammates, fans expect Barcelona to win every tournament and league they play in.

Defenders have a difficult time guarding Iniesta, thanks to skillful moves such as this one.

sent the match into extra time. That's when it became Iniesta's time to shine.

With twenty-six minutes gone in extra time, the Barcelona midfielder scored his second goal of the tournament, giving the victory to the Spaniards. When he took off his jersey and revealed the tribute to his friend Dani Jarque, Iniesta received a yellow-card penalty because the rulebook states that players are not allowed to remove their jerseys. Still, Iniesta was named player of the game. He became an instant hero not only in his country but also across the world.

Winning the World Cup is considered one of the greatest sports achievements because it truly is a world event. In 2010, 204 teams from countries large and small qualified to play in the competition. In the United States—whose team had been eliminated weeks earlier—some twenty-four million people watched the final game on television.

If there was a soccer fan in the world that had not heard of Andrés Iniesta prior to the World Cup, it was a safe bet they knew who he was now.

The loss of former teammate Dani Jarque had a very damaging effect on Iniesta. Jarque was named captain of RCD Espanyol's team a month before his passing.

Europe's Best

Iniesta became a national hero after his World Cup-winning goal. In every game he played in afterwards, he was the star. This was true even when those games were played in opponents' stadiums. In December 2010, for example, Barcelona played a match in Espanyol's stadium. As a *New York Times* reporter wrote, "… it was a player from the visiting team who received the applause of the forty thousand men, women and children in the audience. And then, five minutes before the end, with Espanyol suffering a 5–1 home defeat, its supporters stood to applaud the same Barcelona player in that same spine-tingling manner. This, trust me, is a once in a lifetime thing."

While individual awards are always nice to receive, Iniesta has made it clear that he plays to win trophies like this one, the team trophy for winning the World Cup.

Iniesta and longtime girlfriend Anna Ortiz officially tied the knot on July 8, 2012.

Iniesta finished runner-up in the Ballon d'Or voting in 2010. His Barcelona teammate, Lionel Messi, won the award again. Another Barcelona teammate, Xavi Hernández, finished third.

Iniesta's life changed dramatically on April 3, 2011. That is the day his girlfriend, Anna Ortiz, gave birth to the couple's first daughter. They named her Valeria. Iniesta told *FCBarcelona.com*, "She is someone who has changed my life, filled me with happiness and made me understand things from a different perspective." Iniesta's fans had learned about Ortiz's pregnancy months earlier when Iniesta had written on his Facebook page: "Hi everyone, my future fatherhood has just been reported. I just wanted to confirm the news and tell you that's it's a time filled with happiness for all of us." He also took the opportunity to ask people to respect the couple's privacy. "I hope that you all understand that my partner and I don't want to publicly discuss this issue, which is so marvelous for us."

Iniesta had another special relationship on the soccer field with Xavi Hernández. Hernández was the same height as Iniesta—five-feet, seven-inches—and also played midfield for Barcelona. Many experts believed the two were the greatest midfielder pairing in the world. *The Telegraph* newspaper, in 2012, wrote, "Xavi and Iniesta [are] the exponents of a style that was both revered and apparently invincible. They had cracked football's code, running opponents into the ground, passing in neat triangles out of tight positions and finishing with an artistic flourish."

Iniesta and Hernández had led Barcelona to high league finishes every year they played together. And, in the summer 2012, the pair teamed to help lead Spain's national team to victory in the European Cup, a tournament many consider more difficult to win than the more-popular World Cup. Iniesta was named player of the game several times during the tournament, including in the final match against Italy. For his accomplishments, Iniesta was named the tournament's most valuable player.

The 2012 European Cup was another huge experience for Iniesta. One week after the final match, he experienced an even bigger one. On July 8, 2012, Iniesta and Anna Ortiz—his longtime girlfriend and the mother of his daughter—got married. The wedding was a grand affair. It took place in the gardens of Tamarit Castle, which overlooks the Mediterranean Sea in Tarragona, Spain. Several of Iniesta's Barcelona teammates attended the wedding, including Leo Messi, Gerard Piqué, Víctor Valdés, and Cesc Fàbregas. The same day he was married, Iniesta sent out a message on Twitter to his four million followers: "Amazing day! Just married!" The message was attached to a photo of him and his bride.

Following a honeymoon on the beach in Cancún, Mexico, Iniesta got right back to the world of soccer. That August, he won the Best Player in Europe award. The award was presented to him during a ceremony in

Monaco. His whole family was there to witness, except his dad who did not like to travel on airplanes. True to form, Iniesta gave credit for his award to others: "As I always say, such awards for one individual can't be achieved without the whole team. So it's a sensation that I want to share with my team-mates at the club, and in the national team. It's recognition for the work that you have done well, and that people are proud and have faith in what you do."

Iniesta's exciting 2012 ended with him being named as one of three finalists for the coveted Ballon d'Or. The other two finalists were his teammate Leo Messi and Real Madrid's Cristiano Ronaldo. At the award ceremony in January 2013 in Zurich, Switzerland. Messi was named the winner. Ronaldo finished second and Iniesta was third. It was the fourth year in a row Iniesta had finished fourth or higher for the player of the year award. He was consistently great.

Although he typically lost the Ballon d'Or to flashier players who scored more goals, many insiders believed Iniesta was by far the best player in soccer. Román Riquelme, a former captain of the Argentinian national team, told *FIFA.com*: "The one who plays this game the best is Iniesta: he knows exactly when to go forward and when to drop back. He picks the right moment to do everything: when to dribble, when to speed things up and when to slow things down. And I think that's the only thing that can't be taught or bought."

There is no better ending to a chapter in Iniesta's life than kicking the game-winning goal in the World Cup final.

Returned Blessings

Iniesta is well aware of the fame and fortune soccer has brought him. He has become a world-famous multimillionaire simply playing the game he grew up playing for free next to his family's restaurant in the small Spanish village of Fuentealbilla. But Iniesta has not been spoiled by his success. In fact, he has become well-known over the years for his caring and willingness to help those who have been less fortunate.

In 2009, for example, the mother of a five-year-old Spanish boy with cerebral palsy sent Iniesta a poster and a Barcelona T-shirt for him to sign. She wanted to sell the autographed items to pay for the expensive medical treatments her son needed in the United States. Iniesta immediately signed the items and mailed them to the mother. He also included a special gift. When the mother opened package, she found the yellow and black cleats Iniesta had wore when he scored his famous goal against Chelsea in 2009 in the Champions League semifinal. The shoes were autographed. The sale of the cleats alone raised more than $100,000 for the boy's medical expenses.

Iniesta has done many other good deeds, as well. He has sponsored two children in Peru. He has worked with the Ronald McDonald Foundation charity to help families with children who have cancer. He has worked with the Doctors Without Borders campaign to provide basic medicine to those living in poor countries. He has backed the Spanish Federation for Rare Diseases. He has even helped fellow soccer players.

When Albacete Balompié, the team he played for as a youth, came across difficult financial times, Iniesta purchased a large portion of the team. That gave Albacete Balompié the money to pay its players' salaries and to continue its operation.

"As a person who has been blessed with opportunities, and with the example set by my parents, I assume that my role brings with it some social responsibilities," Iniesta once reported to *totalBarca.com*. "Being a footballer is not only about good passes on the [field]. We have a privileged life, we experience a lot of great things and we must help those most in need."

With determination and hard work like his, there is no doubt that Iniesta will be winning trophies for many years to come.

When his hometown band needed a piano so they could start playing again, Iniesta even bought them one. Today, Fuentealbilla has more than just that piano to show for its hometown hero. Posters, pictures, and other soccer-related memorabilia fill the inside of Iniesta's still-operating family bar. Customers do, too, especially on game days. Many of the bar's visitors are tourists in town to see the bar, Iniesta's home, or to take pictures of themselves next to the larger-than-life World Cup monument with the name "A. Iniesta" stamped across the bottom. Some come to Fuentealbilla just to follow the paths Iniesta once walked. In his hometown, his home country, and even the world, the small soccer player is a big deal.

Career Highlights and Awards

- La Liga champion: 2004–05, 2005–06, 2008–09, 2009–10, 2010–11, 2012–13
- Supercopa de España champion: 2005, 2006, 2009, 2010, 2011
- UEFA Champions League champion: 2005–06, 2008–09, 2010–11
- Copa del Rey champion: 2008–09, 2011–12
- UEFA European Football Championship champion: 2008, 2012
- Don Balón Award: 2008–09
- La Liga's Best Attacking Midfielder: 2008–09, 2010–11, 2011–12
- FIFA Club World Cup champion: 2009, 2011
- FIFA/FIFPro World XI: 2009, 2010, 2011, 2012
- FIFA Puskás Award: Second place in 2009
- UEFA Super Cup champion: 2009, 2011
- UEFA Team of the Year: 2009, 2010, 2011, 2012
- 2010 FIFA World Cup All-Star Team
- Prince of Asturias Award for Sports: 2010 (as member of Spain's national football team)

- FIFA World Cup champion: 2010
- UEFA Euro Player of the Tournament: 2012
- UEFA Best Player in Europe Award: 2012
- IFFHS World's Best Playmaker: 2012
- FIFA Confederations Cup Silver Ball: 2013
- Made his 400th appearance with Barcelona on April 14, 2012
- On April 21, 2012, his record of 55 league games without losing came to an end.

INTERNET ADDRESSES

Official Twitter Page
  <https://twitter.com/andresiniesta8>

Official FC Barcelona Web Site
  <http://www.fcbarcelona.com/>

FIFA Official Site
  <http://www.fifa.com/>

INDEX